I0755970

FINISHING LINE PRESS
www.finishinglinepress.com

Fluent in Silence

poems by

Jayne Shore

Finishing Line Press
Georgetown, Kentucky

Fluent in Silence

ISBN 979-8-89990-437-0 First Edition

Publisher: Leah Huete de Maines
Editor: Christen Kincaid
Cover Art: Kayla Spaeth
Author Photo: Emiliano Morales
Cover Design: Elizabeth Maines McCleavy

Order online: www.finishinglinepress.com
also available on amazon.com

Author inquiries and mail orders:
Finishing Line Press
PO Box 1626
Georgetown, Kentucky 40324
USA

Contents

The Narrows 1

The Midwife 2

Do You Speak Korean? 3

The Blade 4

There is a moment a door remembers being an oak 5

Dawn and We're New 6

Night Theater 7

California Rehabilitation Institute, Room 632 8

Vapor Trail 9

The First Telephone 10

Patient Report 11

After Chronic Pain 12

Coddington Lake 13

I Meet My Mom as a Girl 14

Magnolia Green 15

To My Mom Just Shy of 28 16

The Crossing 17

Notes & Acknowledgments 18

Once I was a wife. Now
I am a wilderness.

—Nancy Miller Gomez

Go where you're wanted.

—Shirley Shore

The Narrows

It's said Denver was carted over
by a band of angels who drunkenly
dropped the city on their way

to Sacramento. I suspect they scraped
their wagon on Longs Peak,
the way it pierces the clouds.

Mom summited
before I was born, slept
in lightning's nursery.

As she descended
along the narrows, I began
as the ache in her foot.

I was made in drought,
the Colorado River running
past like a rumor. Horses

and minnows scattered
across the land, the sun gated off
by the mountains.

Mom stood in the light box
of the kitchen, sculpting
dumplings, pinching closed

their slender peaks.
She had a life before me;
I took it from her.

The Midwife

Sometimes she was the hero, the midwife
of minnows, cupping a tail fin, gently pulling
with Q-tips a baby from its silver mother
until it streamed off to the deep.
Rest your feet now, Mom would say,
lingering in the doorway. *It's time
we both slept.*

Sometimes she showed me
the scar, glinting labrys on her ankle,
from when her aquarium shattered.
How she had tried to carry
the ocean down the stairs.

It was somewhere, past the shards
of her story, paddling on
through forever, that we crossed
like stolen artifacts into America.
We learned to be ordinary,
combed the silt from our hair,
patched our jeans, and memorized
the bus schedule.

Maybe she told me of the peninsula
we came from, its shipyards
and fortress walls, but as I settled
under the covers, her voice
ferrying me toward dreams,
I wasn't awake to hear it.

Do You Speak Korean?

With thanks to Kaveh Akbar

Every morning, I rub the rheum out of my eyes.
My collarbones rest, antlers

fallen from my mother's head. Her hair
gives me away, a dark marquee announcing

I AM FROM ANOTHER WORLD
though I was born here.

Are you Chinese? they ask. And I sing
them Head Shoulders Knees & Toes

in Korean, say I have *two heads,*
one eye, one nose and forget my mouth,

speak *light* and utter
horn, talk of *uncooked rice*

and mean *flesh.*

I was called a doll. I watched other dolls.
They did not speak.

I was called a girl. I watched other girls.
They did not cause a scene

by talking. I became fluent
in silence, the most respected

noise. I was so polite I rubbed myself
out of every room.

The Blade

Katherine said she could teach me to be
like the other girls, pale-faced and prancing
across the ice, wrapping themselves
in tight spins and never dizzying.

In the corner of the rink, she picked up
her skate. She faced me with her blade,
stroked its silver, her bare finger
sliding toward one groove.

This is where you enter
a spin, she said. Promised
beneath my foot, just behind
my toes, was a smooth perfection
where metal and ice give way
to each other, a place
before rust: the sweet spot
of the blade.

I raked my rental skate
across the ice, hoping
to find it. Scarred
the face of the pond, pried

until it cracked.

There is a moment a door remembers being an oak

I came into the world a hatchet

bottle fed fire.
It was the wood

that broke me
set me

in my father's chest
open

to the rain.
I would learn

the language
of rust, be forged

one more life
fastened

to a woman's boot.
I carried

her body
over the frozen lake. She bent

a readied bow
pulled me

behind her head, almost
kissed me.

Dawn and We're New

turning into the rink, our farm town
rapt in factory dreams
while we tie on our skates and drift
onto the ice. Some of us bolt
ahead, lapping each other, passing
our own feet. One of us slips
on her way out the gate.
Another, whipped into a spin,
throws back her head, erecting
with her arms
a whirling crystal ball.
Some of us forgot our clothes
for school. One of us will shatter
her ankle. One will go on
to the Olympics. Some watch
on the sidelines
a bird trapped under the tin roof.
Some have clipped wings,
landing a quarter-turn early,
startled, but a few of us, in our nimble
brawls with gravity,
stand sometimes
on nothing, headhunting
the clouds. We never step off
the ice. We scuff across
the parking lot, backs arched,
blowing holes in our brand new shoes.

Night Theater

She shades me in
with metals and golds,
her brightest yellow
called surrender.
With a brush, she instructs
the light to hold
my face. I don her

peacock blouse.
In the mirror, I almost
recognize myself. We
put on this show
every Friday night, sitting
ankles-crossed
at the bar, negotiating
down the tab
with one voltaic look.

She lends me
wit, teaches me the dance
between strangers.
In the early hours, we scrub
off our glitter, our necks
too tired to hold
up our confident heads.

California Rehabilitation Institute, Room 632

My grandma's eyes, two dulled pearls. She looks through my head and speaks to the ceiling. I look around to see who is in the room.

The cancer, unwelcome in her lungs, has gone like a bad lover to rack her mind and most prized possessions: her words. It's auctioned off each one until I have just a few as parting gifts. *I'll remember who you were in this life,* I say. A promise, not a goodbye.

I'm gonna head out now. I might not see you again for a while. I don't think she understands and I repeat it, but she is asking if we're going to have breakfast at 6 p.m. *Did you move the house?* I know she means the rental car. She is telling me about a beautiful actress who died at 38 of old age and asking, *Will I need a fork in two weeks?* She doesn't know I'm saying goodbye.

Yes, I finally say, *we are going to have breakfast tonight and watch the moon's puppet show moving the tides back and forth. In two weeks, you will need a fork and a spoon.*

I moved the house. I keep moving the house for us.

Vapor Trail

Doctors don't know what to call it: a body
suspended in mid-air, head gracing the ceiling
as I walk across the room. They say I have to
come down from here. Instead, I go out
to join the birds. This is the year
I get good at leaving, practice migrating
past the bar where we met
on 5th Ave. I measure
my distance from home, study the vapor
trails of lanternfish—how they vanish
with their own light.

Haunt me better. Make me beg for another
eight years together.
              It's getting too nice
    all this unbolted sky

              all this room (you threatened)

         to breathe.

The First Telephone

It wasn't invented to call home
to your dad just past curfew
or to send a whisper
in search of a lover's ear.

No, the telephone was meant
to move the walls of the concert hall
across town, trumpets and harps
soon stray in kitchens,
a lone boy's bedroom
one buzzing amphitheater.

I have never put a payphone
to my ear, no, never gone out
to play in the fields
with only the crickets beeping
or fished for a spare nickel
to hear one more *I love you.*

It was this time in November,
the sky rinsed of birds,
when my dad called home
from the hospital. *Grandpa's sick.*
He held the phone up
to his ventilator as we spoke.
Through the walls, through rivers
and towns, his breaths came
as a voice of their own
and I heard him, one last time, sing.

Patient Report

After Nicole Sealey

I'm a mouth breather. My lover said
I talk in my sleep, pleading with angels.
My mom grew up near a nuclear
weapons plant and so I never played
in the mud. There was my great aunt Laura
who had one lung, my grandpa whose hands
quaked in mine. A doctor once threatened
to take my uncle's leg. I sometimes like nectar
and wine as much as they did. Other days,
I can't fathom loving anything, how the heart goes
ambling outside the body. My right ankle clicks
down the stairs. I've bottled rage, uncorked
pleasure. I don't want to stay out of the sun.
My eyes were blue at birth. I had a sister once
in the womb. I came alone today.

After Chronic Pain

What if, after years collapsing
in my ribs, begging
this spine to bend,
it should answer, steady me
before the mailman, a lightning
rod run through me
I move like forgiveness, fall
into a weightless saunter
unbreak all my promises
as if I had not every day
made the vow
to stay a question

Coddington Lake

The speaker is a 400-year-old white pine among the "Lost 40," a strip of forest that was protected from the logging industry in northern Minnesota due to a surveying error. The Public Land Survey in 1882 showed Coddington Lake twice its actual size, effectively hiding 144 acres of trees.

A swan kicked
in me.

I was the stillness
a fisherman sent for, scatterer
of the emeralds in his eyes
before taking his hook
and you ask how I became
so easily the things I feared.

What diamond survives
a ring?

What butterflies stay
on battlefields?

Once the map was wrong
about me, I could be anything—
loon's breath, a doe
bowing to drink her reflection.

I was even lonely in the night,
even safe in the dark.

I Meet My Mom as a Girl

After Nikita Gill

She's written her name on her wrist,
on the inside of her coat, a shield to her
body, carved it in pencils, traced and retraced
it, a wound in her eraser that can't fade
like it does in everyone's ears. She cannot yet say
in America, *That is mine.*

When a girl in a red collared dress
steals her sneakers, I—made of all her words
she did not have—plead: *They're hers. They're hers
so mine,* and she does not walk home that day
barefoot.

Magnolia Green

I'm thinking of the dragonfly
we saw, ornate fossil in the canyon,
a loose stream down its back.
I'm thinking of Palm Springs
before the fires, all the seams and shadows
we came to know in its rock, us looking out
over the splayed roofs, our tawny legs
dipped in the motel pool. It was when
you confessed, *I don't want to be seen*
like this, pulled your shirt
over your bathing suit, got up
from the ledge, never touching
the bottom of that pool as it deepened
to emerald. I wish I had said
you didn't have to be beautiful
to swim among the palms. And we would
float in the verdant shade, gliding
under, kicking up before making
a splash.

To My Mom Just Shy of 28

After Kim Addonizio

If you ever poured beer down
a good man's boots cut
your foot in a hotel pool asked
for a raise and got a hand
up your shirt doctored
your makeup damning the rain put
your heart on trial for wanting
a baby left a white dress
for dead thanked forever
for spitting you back up if
you thought you came
late to the world your father
left / listen I love you
I understand now

The Crossing

The ground was kind.
I walked along the shore, not ready
to know my daughter's name.
Deep in the marble blue
of night, the desert's
wanting. All of us
must weigh the cost
of our dreams.
When monarchs go south
over Lake Superior,
no single generation
makes the journey.

Notes & Acknowledgments

"The Narrows" opens in reference to travel writer Rose Kingsley's observation of Denver: "It was as if the angels were carrying a city to a proper place and accidentally dropped it here."

"I Meet My Mom as a Girl" was published in the *Indianapolis Review.*

Deep gratitude to all the writers and editors who have graced my work. Thank you to my family, my grandmother, and my partner for their support. Special thanks to those in the Sustenance writing community, the Salon, and my editor Rebecca Jamieson for helping me to write this book.

www.ingramcontent.com/pod-product-compliance
Lightning Source LLC
LaVergne TN
LVHW090542110826
845146LV00003B/1240

9798899904370

Jayne Shore is a mixed-race Korean American writer raised in Denver and now living in Minneapolis. She holds an MA from Johns Hopkins University in Science Writing and has published stories of scientists and inventors in outlets such as *Popular Science, Mashable, Psychology Today,* and *STAT News,* as well as poetry in journals including the *Indianapolis Review.* In honor of her late grandmother, she writes under her last name.